K-OFF!

Check out all these stars in your awesome annual!

MATCH OF THE DAY ANNUAL 2012!

LIONEL MESSI

BARCELONA

IN 2011 HE...
Won the Champions League and La Liga to prove he's still the best in the world!

GARETH BALE TOTTENHAM

IN 2011 HE...
Helped Spurs reach the Champions League quarter-finals!

SERGIO AGUERO MAN. CITY

IN 2011 HE...
Became City's latest megabucks signing!

WAYNE ROONEY MAN. UNITED

IN 2011 HE...
Won his fourth Prem trophy in just four years!

TURN OVER NOW!

LADS v DADS!

Superkids spotted!

Hold my hand, son!

This is sooo embarrassing, dad!

EDWIN VAN DER SAR!

JOE VAN DER SAR!

MOTD has uncovered a secret group of superkids trying to outdo their famous dads! Joe van der Sar plays in goal for Man. United's Under-13 team, Isaac Drogba is at Chelsea and 16-year-old Enzo Zidane is tipped to be Real Madrid's next big thing!

GO GET GOTZINHO!

Mario Gotze – known as Gotzinho by his Borussia Dortmund team-mates for his ace dribbling skills – is Man. United's No. 1 transfer target for 2012! The 19-year-old midfielder stormed the Bundesliga and won his first Germany cap last season!

---

3 SUPERKIDS who could join the Prem!

JUAN MANUEL ITURBE

PORTO
Position: Midfielder
Age: 19
Country: Argentina
Top skill: Flying past defenders with his silky skills!
Favourites to sign him: Man. United

CHRISTIAN ERIKSEN

AJAX
Position: Forward
Age: 19
Country: Denmark
Top skill: Setting up goal chances with clever passes around the box!
Favourites to sign him: Man. City

THIAGO ALCANTARA

BARCELONA
Position: Midfielder
Age: 20
Country: Spain
Top skill: Linking up with the midfielders and scoring stunners!
Favourites to sign him: Arsenal

GOSSIP

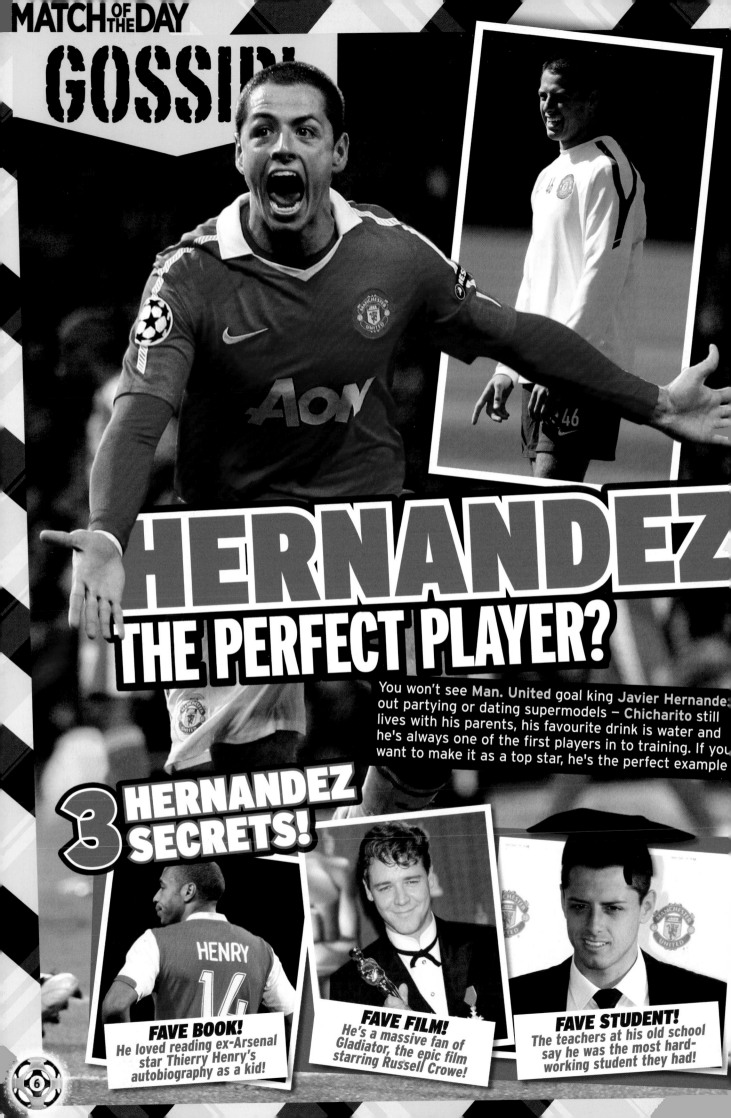

HERNANDEZ
THE PERFECT PLAYER?

You won't see Man. United goal king Javier Hernandez out partying or dating supermodels – Chicharito still lives with his parents, his favourite drink is water and he's always one of the first players in to training. If you want to make it as a top star, he's the perfect example!

3 HERNANDEZ SECRETS!

FAVE BOOK!
He loved reading ex-Arsenal star Thierry Henry's autobiography as a kid!

FAVE FILM!
He's a massive fan of Gladiator, the epic film starring Russell Crowe!

FAVE STUDENT!
The teachers at his old school say he was the most hard-working student they had!

YOU WHAT, CARRA?

You're boss you are, la'!

Eh? I thought Kenny was the boss!

Liverpool's No. 1 striker Luis Suarez has revealed that when he first moved to Anfield, he couldn't understand a word of the Scouse accent! He says Jamie Carragher was the hardest to understand!

MOTD can reveal that Arsenal hero Jack Wilshere says he'd use the name Jack-in-the-box if he was a professional wrestler. Erm, that doesn't sound scary to us, mate!

JACK-IN-A-BOX!

SERGIO SEES RED!

Sergio Aguero is a megastar at Man. City now, but his first game in England saw him sent of in a UEFA Cup game against Bolton!

Off you go!

Come on, ref!

FIRST CARS OF THE STARS!

Hey, don't laugh!

JAMES MILNER
MAN. CITY
FORD FOCUS

JACK RODWELL
EVERTON
AUDI A3

WAYNE ROONEY
MAN. UNITED
FORD KA

SPOT THE BALL!

15 POINTS for each right answer!

There are too many balls in these footy pics! Can you spot the real one in each?

STEVEN GERRARD

LIVERPOOL & ENGLAND

POSITION: Midfielder
AGE: 31
VALUE: £15 million
DID YOU KNOW?
Stevie G has won the Champions League, the UEFA Cup and two FA Cups with Liverpool!

MATCH OF THE DAY

BIGGEST
BUST

Hey, get a grip, JT!

Arm wrestler!

TIM CAHILL v JOHN TERRY

Scary Skrtel!

Watch out Martin, Shorty is gonna charge!

RAFAEL v MARTIN SKRTEL & LUCAS

I'm louder than you are!

Shouting match!

Never! Raaaaahh!

GARY TAYLOR-FLETCHER v ZAT KNIGHT

Let's all pinch him, lads!

Can't feel a thing!

MARIO BALOTELLI v MAN. UNITED

Brave Balotelli!

PREMIER LEAGUE 2011
TEAM OF THE YEAR!

MOTD picks our Premier League Team Of The Year – find out who's made it in!

THE KEEPER!

JOE HART
MAN. CITY

MOTD SAYS: The big City keeper is the man MOTD picks to stop the goals going in. Hart won his first trophy in 2011 when Man. City won the FA Cup and he was also awarded the Barclays Golden Glove trophy after keeping 18 clean sheets!

LEFT-BACK!

LEIGHTON BAINES EVERTON

MOTD SAYS: Are you surprised that Baines is our No.1 left-back? Well, you shouldn't be because he's had a storming 2011. Leighton's left foot is one of the best in the Premier League and last season he scored seven goals in all competitons – including stunning free-kicks against Spurs and Chelsea!

CENTRE-BACK!

NEMANJA VIDIC MAN. UNITED

MOTD SAYS: The Prem Team Of The Year just has to have the Man. United captain in defence! Leading his team to another title and the Champions League final in 2011, Vidic makes brave blocks and tackles and then bursts forward to smash home a bullet header!

CENTRE-BACK!

VINCENT KOMPANY MAN. CITY

MOTD SAYS: Getting the ball past Kompany is more difficult than your maths homework! The Man. City giant is as big as Didier Drogba, faster than Luis Suarez and has slick skills like Rio Ferdinand. He made the 2011 PFA Team Of The Year and the MOTD boys think he's a top-class defender!

RIGHT-BACK!

GLEN JOHNSON LIVERPOOL

MOTD SAYS: The Liverpool and England ace really hit top gear after Kenny Dalglish took over at Anfield. We knew the 27-year-old was a class athlete with the defensive skills and attacking brain you need to be a modern full-back, but he's even played left-back to show how versatile he is!

TURN OVER FOR MORE STARS!

MIDFIELDER!

GARETH BALE
TOTTENHAM

MOTD SAYS: Playing Bale on the left of our midfield trio means his deadly mix of speed, stamina and shooting will rip defenders to pieces. The Spurs star can be unstoppable when he's in the mood – him and Baines on the left is an awesome combination!

MIDFIELDER!

JACK WILSHERE ARSENAL

MOTD SAYS: Every top team needs a world-class midfielder who's comfortable on the ball, quick thinking, spots the best pass and bosses the middle of the pitch. Jack is one of the world's top teenagers and walks into **MOTD**'s line-up!

MIDFIELDER!

ASHLEY YOUNG MAN. UNITED

MOTD SAYS: Young could play on the left, the right or behind the strikers in **MOTD**'s attacking team! He was one of Villa's best players last season – and since joining Man. United in the summer he's looked even hotter!

STRIKER!

WAYNE ROONEY MAN. UNITED

MOTD SAYS: Rooney had a slow start last season, but he hit back to help United lift another league title. Expect him to fire The Red Devils to more glory this season and to pick up more silverware!

STRIKER!

JAVIER HERNANDEZ MAN. UNITED

MOTD SAYS: Rooney's strike partner rightly takes his place in this all-star line-up. He's clever, quick, a good team player – but most importantly he can stick the ball in the net with his eyes closed. He's already a Man. United hero!

STRIKER!

LUIS SUAREZ LIVERPOOL

MOTD SAYS: The tricky striker has only been in the Premier League since January, but he's such a talent that we just had to pick him with Rooney and Hernandez! Suarez is such a danger in the box and works hard for the team to set up chances and put pressure on defenders!

TURN OVER TO PICK YOUR DREAM TEAM!

2011 TEAM OF THE YEAR!

THIS IS THE MOTD TEAM OF THE YEAR, BUT YOU CAN PICK YOURS TOO!

HERNANDEZ

SUAREZ

ROONEY

WILSHERE

BALE

YOUNG

VIDIC

KOMPANY

BAINES

HART

JOHNSON

YOU CAN CHOOSE FROM...

KEEPERS!
Joe Hart
Pepe Reina
David de Gea
Petr Cech
Mark Schwarzer
Tim Howard
Brad Friedel

LEFT-BACKS!
Leighton Baines
Patrice Evra
Jose Enrique
Ashley Cole
B. Assou-Ekotto
Maynor Figueroa
Fabio

RIGHT-BACKS!
Glen Johnson
Rafael
Bacary Sagna
Micah Richards
Kyle Walker
Martin Kelly
Branislav Ivanovic

write your team's name here!

CENTRE-BACKS!
Nemanja Vidic
Vincent Kompany
Michael Dawson
John Terry
Rio Ferdinand
Phil Jagielka
Jamie Carragher

MIDFIELDERS!
Jack Wilshere
Gareth Bale
Ashley Young
Luka Modric
Frank Lampard
Lucas
Yaya Toure

KEEPER

LEFT-BACK

RIGHT-BACK

CENTRE-BACK

CENTRE-BACK

CENTRE-MIDFIELDER

CENTRE-MIDFIELDER

CENTRE-MIDFIELDER

STRIKERS!
Wayne Rooney
Javier Hernandez
Luis Suarez
Robin van Persie
Sergio Aguero
Andy Carroll
Darren Bent

STRIKER

STRIKER

STRIKER

WAYNE ROONEY

MAN. UNITED & ENGLAND

POSITION: Striker
AGE: 25
VALUE: £50 million
DID YOU KNOW?
Wazza has won four Prem titles, two League Cups and a Champions League with United!

MATCH OF THE **DAY**

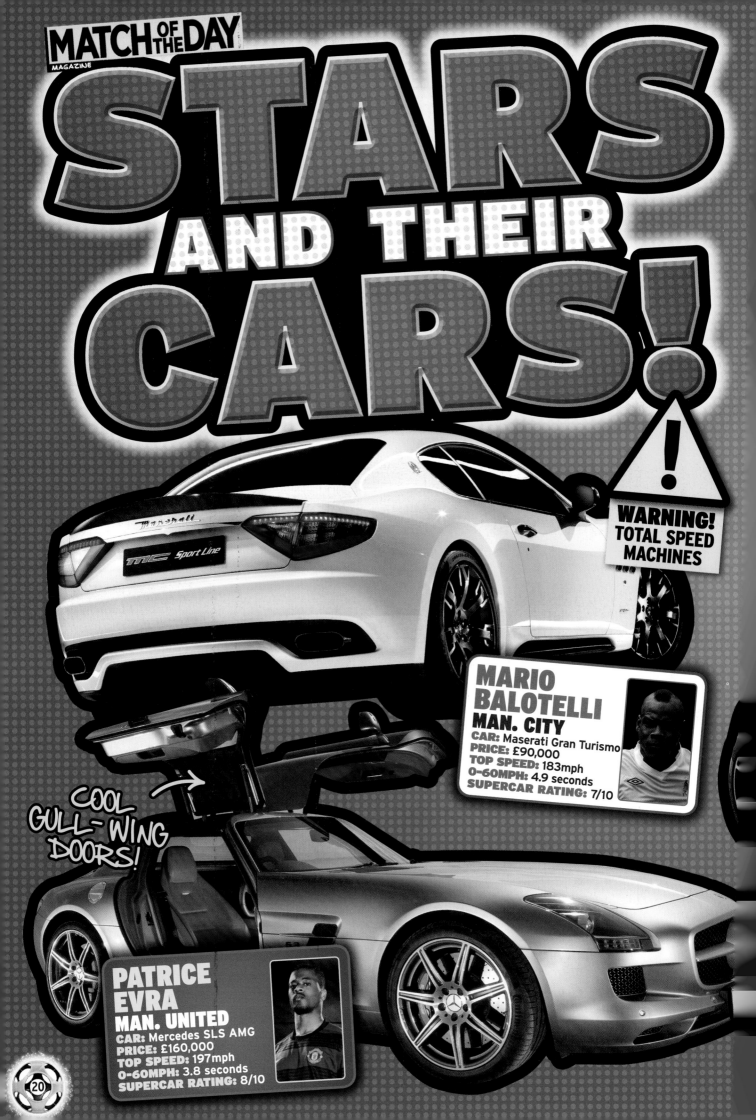

STARS
AND THEIR
CARS!

WARNING!
TOTAL SPEED
MACHINES

Maserati
MC Sport Line

MARIO BALOTELLI
MAN. CITY
CAR: Maserati Gran Turismo
PRICE: £90,000
TOP SPEED: 183mph
0-60MPH: 4.9 seconds
SUPERCAR RATING: 7/10

COOL GULL-WING DOORS!

PATRICE EVRA
MAN. UNITED
CAR: Mercedes SLS AMG
PRICE: £160,000
TOP SPEED: 197mph
0-60MPH: 3.8 seconds
SUPERCAR RATING: 8/10

DAVID DE GEA
MAN. UNITED
CAR: Audi RS5
PRICE: £60,000
TOP SPEED: 155mph
0-60MPH: 4.6 seconds
SUPERCAR RATING: 6/10

JUST LIKE JAMES BOND!

JERMAINE PENNANT
STOKE
CAR: Aston Martin DBS
PRICE: £170,000
TOP SPEED: 191mph
0-60MPH: 3.9 seconds
SUPERCAR RATING: 9/10

THEO WALCOTT
ARSENAL
CAR: Mercedes SL65 AMG
PRICE: £250,000
TOP SPEED: 199mph
0-60MPH: 3.9 seconds
SUPERCAR RATING: 9/10

WARNING!
TOTAL SPEED MACHINES

LOUIS SAHA
EVERTON
CAR: Ferrari 458 Italia
PRICE: £160,000
TOP SPEED: 202mph
0-60MPH: 3.4 seconds
SUPERCAR RATING: 9/10

FLASH FERRARI!

21

FRANK LAMPARD

CHELSEA & ENGLAND

POSITION: Midfielder
AGE: 33
VALUE: £10 million
DID YOU KNOW?
Frank has scored more goals for Chelsea than any other midfielder in the club's history!

MATCH OF THE DAY

Your ultimate guide to...
MATCH OF THE

LONDON!

MANCHESTER

MANCHESTER MOVE!
MOTD is filmed in the BBC's Television Centre in west London, but at the end of 2011 it'll move to a flash new studio in Manchester's Salford Quays!

Ha-ha! That tickles!

GOING LIVE!
Match of the Day is always broadcast live, which means there's a lot of work to do after the games finish on Saturday night before the show goes out in the evening!

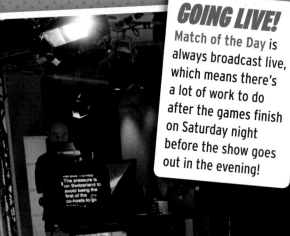

MAKE-UP OF THE DAY!
All the MOTD experts have a bit of make-up on their faces to stop the studio lights shining off them. Alan Shearer has a brush-up here!

Your ultimate guide to...
MATCH OF THE DAY

DIXON!

LAWRENSON

DOUBLE TROUBLE!
Match of the Day always has two footy experts talking about the action with Gary. Watch out for Lee Dixon, Mark Lawrenson, Shearer and Hansen in the studio this season!

TV CRAZY!
The MOTD boys will spend all Saturday afternoon watching live footy on all these TVs! They make lots of notes so they can chat about the action on the programme later!

WORLD STARS!
Match of the Day's coverage of the World Cup finals is always amazing. Check out the guys showing off their studio at the 2010 finals in South Africa!

Stay up late to watch me!

MURRAY!

SUNDAY SERVICE!

Match of the Day 2 goes out on Sunday nights and has been on air since 2004. Colin Murray has presented it since 2010 – he's a Liverpool fan and loves it when The Reds win!

Robinson

Murphy

MOTTY'S A LEGEND!

John Motson has been commentating on footy games for MOTD for more than 40 years. Here he is with Lawro at the Euro 2008 finals in Germany!

GUEST APPEARANCES!

Prem stars often make guest appearances on MOTD2. Last season, Danny Murphy and Paul Robinson were in the studio!

PRIZE TIME!

Since 1970, Match of the Day has picked a Goal of the Month winner and a Goal of the Season too. In 2011, Rooney's ace overhead kick against Man. City was their top choice!

27

BEST PLAYER!

LIONEL MESSI, BARCELONA

It just had to be him, didn't it? No other man on the planet can touch Messi's awesome skills!

BEST TRANSFER!

I've got cash left over for sweets!

LUIS SUAREZ, LIVERPOOL

Liverpool paid Ajax a bargain £22.8m for the red-hot Uruguay striker – he's whacking in goals and the fans love him!

Pick that one out of the net!

BEST GOAL!

WAYNE ROONEY, MAN. UNITED

Rooney's overhead kick winner against Man. City in the Premier League was just incredible!

BIGGEST LAUGH!

Err, you might want to change!

SURMAN'S SHORTS SHOCK

While Norwich were celebrating getting promoted, Andrew Surman had his shorts pulled down – and fans saw his grundies!

AWARDS! 2011!

BEST GAME!

Who wants to give me a cuddle?

MAN. UNITED V MAN. CITY, COMMUNITY SHIELD
The Community Shield is usually well boring, but this one was a classic. Man. United were 2-0 down, but stormed back to win 3-2 at Wembley!

BIGGEST JOKER!

MARIO BALOTELLI, MAN. CITY
The City star is always up for a laugh – pranking team-mates, messing about on the pitch, wearing dodgy hats and loads more!

Do you like my new home kit?

BEST BOOTS!

ADIDAS F50 ADIZERO PRIME
It was close, because we love the Puma, Umbro and Nike boots, but the Adidas F50 AdiZero Prime are so sick!

BIGGEST LOSER!

Shhh! Don't tell everyone, MOTD!

BEBE, MAN. UNITED
Sir Alex splashed out £7m on the striker who nobody had ever heard of – he was so rubbish that he was sent out on loan!

MESSI

11 amazing things you didn't know about him!

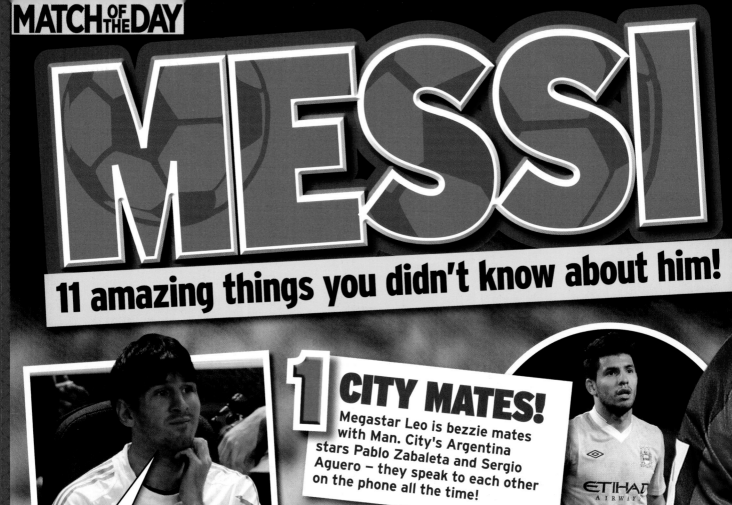

What's 2+2? Err, I dunno!

1 CITY MATES!

Megastar Leo is bezzie mates with Man. City's Argentina stars Pablo Zabaleta and Sergio Aguero – they speak to each other on the phone all the time!

2 SCHOOL SUCKS!

Messi wasn't too hot at school – in fact, his best mate used to write the answers on the back of his rubber and pass them to Leo when the teacher wasn't looking!

3 OLD BOYS FAVES!

Leo signed for his boyhood club Newell's Old Boys when he was just seven – but did you know his dad and two brothers had already played for the club as well?

4 COMPUTER STAR!

The attacking genius likes to play PES with his footy mates – and he's featured on the cover of the game!

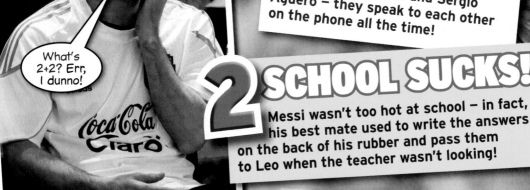

5 BARCA'S MEAL DEAL!

The Barcelona bosses were so keen to make sure they didn't miss out on the world's top teenager in 2000, they used a napkin in a restaurant as a contract!

6 BOOTING IT!

Messi is famous for wearing these wicked Adidas boots for Barcelona – but he used to wear Nike when he was a youngster at the club!

7 NOT AS HOT AS ROD!

Wigan striker Hugo Rodallega once said that he's definitely better than Messi after scoring more goals than him at a South American youth tournament in 2005!

8 MESSI BEEFS UP!

Leo's favourite food is beef steak covered in breadcrumbs. When his mum comes to visit from Argentina, she spends the whole day cooking it so his fridge is well stocked up!

You're not meant to kick me, bruv!

9 HIS BIG BROTHER!

His team-mate Gerard Pique is like his big brother in the Barcelona squad – if Leo gets kicked out on the pitch, Pique is straight over to stick up for him!

10 GREAT GRANDMA!

Messi's grandma used to take him to all his training sessions, but when the coaches said he was too small to play she argued with them to let him on the pitch!

Put me down, Cesc!

11 LEO THE FAB LITTLE LAD!

Cesc Fabregas was in the same Barça youth team as Leo – the ex-Arsenal midfielder says that Messi used to be very quiet and shy!

PREMIER LEAGUE ZOO!

IF PREM CLUBS WERE ANIMALS...

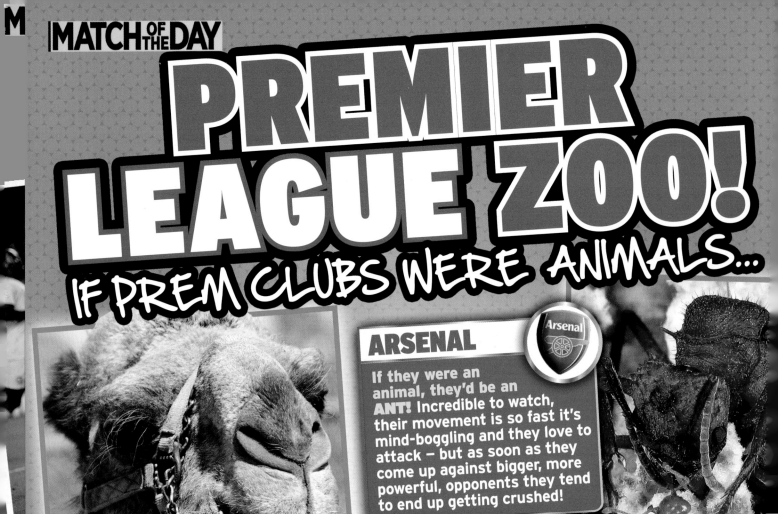

ARSENAL

If they were an animal, they'd be an **ANT!** Incredible to watch, their movement is so fast it's mind-boggling and they love to attack — but as soon as they come up against bigger, more powerful, opponents they tend to end up getting crushed!

I've got the hump!

STOKE

If they were an animal, they'd be a **CAMEL!** They're big, powerful and will always work hard for their boss. There's nothing pretty about them and they've got a bit of a nasty streak — so be careful!

BLACKBURN

If they were an animal, they'd be a **CRAB!** Tough little cookies who love a good scrap — maybe that's why they don't have many fans? But their biggest weakness is they struggle going forwards!

Up The Toon!

WIGAN

If they were an animal, they'd be a **HEDGEHOG!** Nobody has a bad word to say about them! They're small, not very threatening — but they do have a habit of rolling over if they're attacked!

NEWCASTLE

If they were an animal, they'd be a **PENGUIN!** Famous for their black and white colours, they're always entertaining to watch and attract big crowds — but you can guarantee that they'll suffer an epic slip-up sooner or later!

RYAN GIGGS QUIZ!

Giggsy heads into 2012 having won the Prem 12 times! Take on these ten teasers!

1 In which year did Giggsy make his United debut?
A 1986 B 1991 C 1996

2 Who did he win his first Champions League against in 1999?
A Bayern Munich
B Chelsea
C Valencia

3 What is his middle name?
A Joseph
B Toby
C Oserus

4 What shirt number does he wear at United?
A No.7
B No.11
C No.14

2 POINTS for each correct answer!

5 When was he named BBC Sports Personality of the Year?
A 2009 B 2010 C 2011

6 How many United mangers has he played under?
A 1 B 2 C 3

7 Which country did he used to play for?
A England
B Wales
C Ireland

8 When is Giggsy's birthday?
A February
B July
C November

9 Which trophy hasn't he won?
A FA Cup B Carling Cup
C Europa League

10 Giggs trained with Man. City as a schoolboy – true or false!
A True
B False

MY SCORE OUT OF 20

(DON'T CHEAT!)

ANSWERS 1B 2A 3A 4B 5A 6A 7B 8C 9C 10A

MORE QUIZ FUN ON PAGE 54!

SERGIO AGUERO

MAN CITY & ARGENTINA

POSITION: Striker
AGE: 23
VALUE: £40 million
DID YOU KNOW?
Aguero scored twice on his Premier League debut for Man. City this season!

MATCH OF THE DAY

M MESSI

This guy has been on another planet in 2011. In fact, we think he plays his footy in a different galaxy these days! Messi scooped the World Player Of The Year award and he tore Man. United to pieces in the Champions League final. We worship him!

"Here we go, Paz!"

P PAZ & BEZ

MOTD's wicked reporters met up with all the big stars in 2011! They even spent the summer in Africa with Arsenal and Switzerland centre-back Johan Djourou!

"Yeah, winners only!"

"Hands off, Bebe!"

N NINETEEN

That's the number of league titles Man. United now have, after lifting the Prem trphy in May – beating Liverpool's 18!

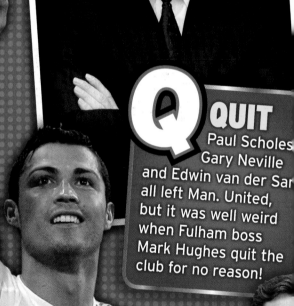

Q QUIT

Paul Scholes, Gary Neville and Edwin van der Sar all left Man. United, but it was well weird when Fulham boss Mark Hughes quit the club for no reason!

"Love the shirt!"

O OVERHEAD KICK

Do you remember when Wayne Rooney smashed in this beauty against Man. City? Turn to page 56 now to learn how you can pull off this amazing skill too!

R RONALDO

The Real Madrid goal machine set a new scoring record in Spain. He notched 40 La Liga goals and an amazing 53 in all competitions for Madrid!

S SPAIN

We bet that if the Spanish entered the world ballet championships, they'd win that too! Their under-21 team also won the Euro finals in Denmark in 2011!

W WILSHERE

What a year it was for the young Arsenal and England midfielder! He was named the PFA Young Player Of The Year and is now the first name on Wenger's teamsheet!

T TOP TV

Watching Match of the Day on Saturday night, or the repeat on Sunday morning, gives you the perfect footy fix at the weekend!

X X-RATED

You can be sure there'll always be some big bust-ups on the pitch! We reckon the Manchester derbies saw most of the meaty action in 2011!

U URUGUAY

Forget Brazil, Argentina, Paraguay, Chile and Mexico, Uruguay were better than them all in the 2011 Copa America finals. Luis Suarez's team lifted the big trophy back in July!

Y YOUNG

Ashley Young wasted no time in getting his Man. United career off to a cracking start after joining from Aston Villa!

I'm red-hot Ash!

V VILLAS-BOAS

Had you heard of this guy before he became the new Chelsea boss in the summer? Probably not, but Andre used to coach at Chelsea years ago – and now he's back, this time in the hot seat!

Z ZAMORA

The Fulham striker scored on his Premier League return after a five month injury and then made it back into the England squad!

10 REASONS WHY WE LOVE...
EURO 2012!

MOTD reveals why next summer's Euro 2012 finals will be awesome!

1 NEW STARS!
Every country will have a wonderkid on show at the tournament – Spain's Juan Mata and Germany's Mario Gotze could become megastars. Watch out for the youngsters ripping it up in June and July!

2 THE JOINT HOSTS!
This is only the second time Poland have made it to the European Championships – and it's Ukraine's first! That means the hosts will be going absolutely mental, turning the festival of footy into one great big Euro party!

3 BONKERS FRANCE!
Nobody gave us as many LOLs at a footy tournament as France did in the 2010 World Cup – Anelka was sent home, the squad went on strike and Evra made the fitness coach cry – what crazy stuff will they get up to this time around?

4 FOOTY ON TV!
Euro 2012 is going to be a total TV festival – you'll be able to watch the action for four weeks! Gary Lineker and the Match of the Day boys will be at the tournament to bring you every kick!

5 SWEET STADIUMS!
Six new stadiums have been knocked up especially for the tournament, but our favourite is easily Shakhtar Donetsk's Donbass Arena in Ukraine. It cost £242 million, holds 50,000 fans and looks like a flying saucer!

6 SUPER SPAIN!
All eyes will be on the reigning World and Euro champions in Poland & Ukraine. They've got amazing strikers, awesome keepers and the greatest midfield on the planet – can anyone stop them?

7 THE WINNERS!
It's the moment 16 countries will be dreaming of at the start of the tournament – but only one can enjoy! Nothing beats the feeling of lifting that trophy and officially being the best footy country in Europe!

8 UNDERDOG SHOCKS!
There's always one nation that takes a tournament by storm, stringing together a run of crazy results and upsets! Think Ghana at the last World Cup and Russia in Euro 2008. In Euro 2004, Greece went all the way – who will it be this time?

9 MIDFIELD MAGICIANS!
It used to be all about the strikers, but midfielders are now the biggest stars in footy! Players like Wesley Sneijder will be busting out their world-class skills, dribbling and passing to make next summer one of the hottest ever!

10 MOTD MAG!
Don't miss Match of the Day magazine every Tuesday before, during and after the tournament! We'll have all the biggest Euro 2012 stars, the latest news, gossip, wicked team guides and loads more from the finals!

NAME THE TEAM!

Which Prem club have all these top stars played for in the past?

JOLEON LESCOTT
MAN. CITY

MARCO MATERAZZI
INTER MILAN

25 POINTS for the right answer!

SIMON DAVIES
FULHAM

THE TEAM IS...

GARY NAYSMITH
HUDDERSFIELD

LANDON DONOVAN
LA GALAXY

WAYNE ROONEY
MAN. UNITED

62

(DON'T CHEAT!)

MY SCORE OUT OF 25

ANSWER Everton

MORE QUIZ FU ON PAGE

ALEXANDRE PATO

AC MILAN & BRAZIL

POSITION: Striker
AGE: 22
VALUE: £20 million
DID YOU KNOW?
Pato scored 14 goals as Milan won the Italian league title last season!

MATCH OF THE DAY

**1992-1993
MAN. UNITED**

First Prem winners!

**1993-1994
MAN. UNITED**

Champions! Champions!

**1994-1995
BLACKBURN**

MOTD's Alan Shearer!

MATCH OF THE DAY

20 PREM Y

**2012 is the 20th year of the Premier League
– take a look at all the title winners!**

**1999-2000
MAN. UNITED**

Can someone help me lift this thing?

**2000-2001
MAN. UNITED**

**2001-2002
ARSENAL**

This is shinier than my head!

**2002-2003
MAN. UNITED**

**2005-2006
CHELSEA**

Shall we let someone else win this?

Yeah, I'm bored of winning!

**2006-2007
MAN. UNITED**

**2007-2008
MAN. UNITED**

64

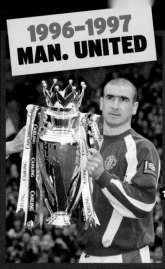
1995-1996
MAN. UNITED

I'll be back for you next year!

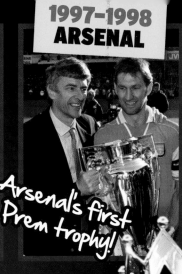
1996-1997
MAN. UNITED

1997-1998
ARSENAL

Arsenal's first Prem trophy!

1998
MAN. U

EARSI

First one for The Blues!

2003-2004
ARSENAL

2004-2005
CHELSEA

United rule the Prem – again!

Three in a row for United!

2008-2009
MAN. UNITED

2009-2010
CHELSEA

United' 12th Pre crown

2010-2011
MAN. UNITE

MATCH OF THE DAY QUIZ!
GUESS THE SCORE!

Can you remember the final score from these big games this year?

1 CHAMPIONS LEAGUE FINAL
Barcelona ☐ - 1 Man. United

2 PREMIER LEAGUE
Newcastle 4 - ☐ Arsenal

3 COMMUNITY SHIELD
Man. United 3 - ☐ Man. City

4 CHAMPIONSHIP PLAY-OFF FINAL
Reading 2 - ☐ Swansea

10 POINTS for each correct answer!

MORE QUIZ FU ON PAGE 7

ANSWERS 1 Barcelona 3-1 Man. United, 2 Newcastle 4-4 Arsenal, 3 Man. United 3-2 Man. City, 4 Reading 2-4 Swansea

MY SCORE OUT OF 40 ☐

FRANCK RIBERY

BAYERN MUNICH & FRANCE

POSITION: Forward
AGE: 28
VALUE: £30 million
DID YOU KNOW?
Franck has won both the French Player Of The Year and German Player Of The Year awards!

MATCH OF THE DAY

MATCH OF THE DAY
KICKABOUT
HOW TO BE A FOOTBALL TV PRESENTER!
By MOTD's Ore Oduba

1 LOVE YOUR FOOTBALL!

ORE SAYS: "Live it, eat it, read it (in MOTD magazine!) and breathe football. You don't necessarily have to have played professionally, but you have to know your stuff. The best football presenters are big fans of the game!"

2 PRACTICE MAKES PERFECT!

ORE SAYS: "You can have a go at presenting wherever you are and the more you do it, the better you'll get. Do it in front of the mirror or get a mate to record you on camera. It might sound and feel silly, but it should help build your confidence on screen!"

Smile for the camera!

Ore in action!

3 GET CREATIVE!

ORE SAYS: "Ideas are a big part of TV so get creative! Start a blog about things in football that interested you. Or start a video blog. It can basically be your own footy show!"

4 WORK EXPERIENCE!

ORE SAYS: "Without it, getting into telly is pretty tricky. There's so much more to TV than just presenting, so it's good to show you know how it all works. And it's not just TV experience that helps – radio, papers and the internet are big parts of media!"

5 BE YOURSELF!

ORE SAYS: "One of the reasons we enjoy watching our favourite presenters is because they're being themselves – it's what makes them unique. Don't copy what you think makes a good presenter, instead do it in your own style and be yourself!"

Watch Ore on MOTD Kickabout every Saturday morning CBBC and BBC 2

ROBINHO

AC MILAN & BRAZIL

POSITION: Striker
AGE: 27
VALUE: £20 million
DID YOU KNOW?
Robinho has won league titles in Brazil, Italy and Spain – and the Copa America with Brazil!

MATCH OF THE DAY

MEGA MA

Match of the Day reveals the best games to look out for in 2012!

CHAMPIONSHIP PLAY-OFF FINAL

npower CHAMPIONSHIP

The Championship is the most unpredictable league in the world. Who will reach the final and get a shot at making the Prem?

SUPER STAT: The finalists usually agree to give money from ticket sales to the losing team!

PLAY-OFF FINAL WINNERS 2011

Shot at the Prem!

WINNER 2011 SWANSEA CITY

19 MAY

ARSENAL v TOTTENHAM

Derby battle!

25 FEBRUARY

This match is not just a North London derby any more – it's now an epic clash in the chase for a top-four finish!

SUPER STAT: Spurs came from 2-0 down to win 3-2 at the Emirates last season!

BARCLAYS PREMIER LEAGUE

FA CUP FINAL

Man. City scooped the FA Cup last May, but who will lift the trophy next year at Wembley? All the Prem's big boys will fancy their chances!

SUPER STAT: Manchester United have won the FA Cup a record 11 times!

15 MAY

MAN. CITY v MAN. UNITED

The Manchester derby has never been so close. With one month until the end of the season, this could decide the title!

SUPER STAT: Only two goals have been scored in the last three league meetings at the Etihad Stadium!

28 APRIL

BARCLAYS PREMIER LEAGUE

CHELSEA v MAN. UNITED

BARCLAYS PREMIER LEAGUE

Whoever wins this will give their title hopes a massive boost!

SUPER STAT: Man. United haven't won at Stamford Bridge in the Premier League since 2002!

Massive match-up!

4 FEBRUARY

BARCELONA v REAL MADRID

Real Madrid got tonked 5-0 at the Nou Camp in the league last season and they want revenge!

SUPER STAT: These sides met five times last season, because they kept drawing each other in cups!

22 APRIL

LFP

TCHES! 2012

25 FEBRUARY

LIVERPOOL v EVERTON

Everton haven't won at Anfield in the league since 1999 and they want to change that!
SUPER STAT: No other fixture has had more red cards since the Premier League started!

CARLING CUP FINAL

The first silverware of the season is up for grabs, and a place in Europe for the winners!
SUPER STAT: Liverpool have won the League Cup seven times – that's more than any other club!

First final of the year!

CARLING CUP

26 FEBRUARY

Kings of Europe!

CHAMPIONS LEAGUE FINAL

19 MAY

No club has been European champions two years in a row since way back in 1990. Can Barça defend their crown in the final in Munich?
SUPER STAT: Nottingham Forest won the European Cup in 1979 and 1980!

1 JULY

EURO 2012 POLAND-UKRAINE

EURO 2012 FINAL

Euro 2012 will take place in Poland and Ukraine, with Poland kicking off the tournament on 8 June and Ukraine hosting the big final on 1 July!
SUPER STAT: Fernando Torres got the winner for Spain in the 2008 final against Germany!

Fixtures subject to change

MATCH OF THE DAY QUIZ! REAL MADRID QUIZ!

Answer these **ten** well tasty questions on La Liga's most successful ever club. Ole!

1 How many times have Real Madrid won the Spanish league?
A 8 B 19 C 31

2 Which Prem side did Jose Mourinho used to manage?
A Liverpool
B Chelsea
C Man. City

3 What is Real's stadium called?
A Santiago Bernabeu
B Nou Camp
C San Siro

4 What number does Sergio Ramos wear?
A No.4
B No.14
C No.24

5 When was the last time Real won the Champions League?
A 1988 B 2002 C 2011

6 Which Real star has the most Spain caps?
A Iker Casillas
B Sergio Ramos
C Raul Albiol

7 Which Prem club has Xabi Alonso played for?
A Swansea
B Newcastle
C Liverpool

2 POINTS for each correct answer!

8 Who do they play the match known as El Classico against?
A Atletico Madrid
B Barcelona
C Malaga

9 Which country does midfielder Mesut Ozil play for?
A France
B Portugal
C Germany

10 Man. City signed Sergio Aguero from Real Madrid!
A True   B False

MY SCORE OUT OF 20

ANSWERS 1C 2B 3A 4A 5B 6A 7C 8B 9C 10B

(DON'T CHEAT!) MORE QUIZ FUN ON PAGE 80

74

ASHLEY YOUNG

MAN. UNITED & ENGLAND

POSITION: Forward
AGE: 26
VALUE: £28 million
DID YOU KNOW?
Ashley won the 2009 PFA Young Player Of The Year award while playing for Aston Villa!

MATCH OF THE DAY

SPOT IN 2012!

Tick these off once you see them happen!

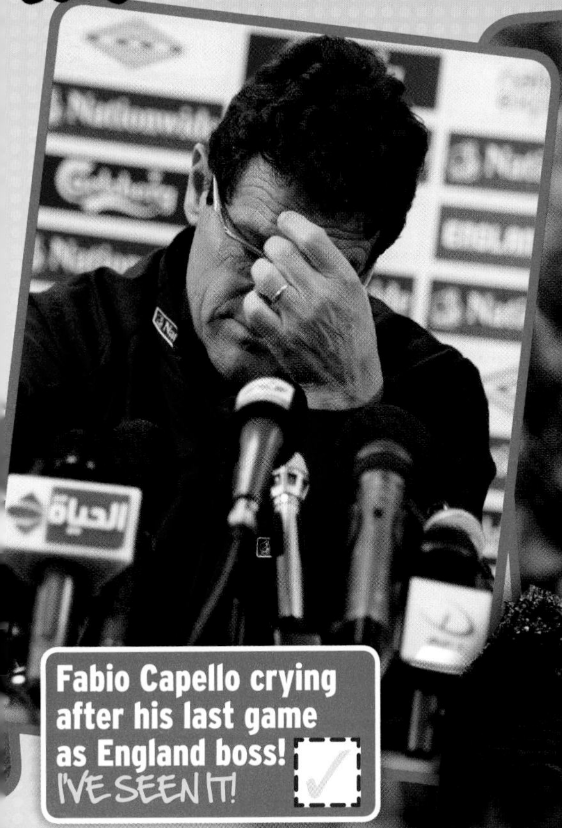

Fabio Capello crying after his last game as England boss! **I'VE SEEN IT!** ✓

No way, Cher Lloyd rocks!

Justin Bieber's the best!

BALOTELLI 45

Mario Balotelli arguing with his manager! **I'VE SEEN IT!** ✓

I want a yes from the judges!

tombola

Mad new look for Andy?

But I asked for a Fellaini, dude!

Standard Chartered

Asamoah Gyan dancing after scoring a goal! **I'VE SEEN IT!** ✓

Andy Carroll with a new hairstyle! **I'VE SEEN IT!** ✓

1 THE MANAGER
SIR ALEX FERGUSON
In his 25 years at Old Trafford, he's won two Champions Leagues, 12 Premier League titles, a Cup Winners' Cup, five FA Cups, four League Cups and ten Community/Charity Shields!

2 THE PLAYERS
BARCELONA
We need a starting line-up to strike fear into the opposition – and even our gran knows that Barça, with Messi, Xavi and Iniesta, are head and shoulders above everyone else!

Look mean and tough, boys!

ULTIMATE FC

Ever wondered what would make up the perfect football club? Well, wonder no more...

3 THE STADIUM
NOU CAMP
This is the biggest and most spectacular football stadium in Europe. It holds 98,000 and if you're sat in the top tier, it feels like your head is in the clouds!

4 THE HISTORY
REAL MADRID
The ultimate club needs an awesome history – and histories don't come any more amazing than Real Madrid's. They've been European champions a record nine times, and won La Liga 31 times – ten more than Barcelona!

5 THE OWNER
SHEIKH MANSOUR
Say hello to one of the richest men in football. Since buying Man. City three years ago, he's spent almost £400 million on players, turning them from chumps into potential champs!

Wave if you have stacks of cash!

6 THE FANS
BOCA JUNIORS
We need some wild, noisy and bonkers fans to fill the ground every week to inspire our team to victory. Boca's passionate fans will do that job perfectly!

We're bonkers for Boca!

CRISTIANO RONALDO

REAL MADRID & PORTUGAL

POSITION: Forward
AGE: 26
VALUE: £90 million
DID YOU KNOW?
Ronaldo became the world's most expensive player when Real paid £80 million for him!

MATCH OF THE DAY

MATCH OF THE DAY QUIZ!

SPOT THE DIFFERENCE!

Get **two points** for each of the **five** changes you spot in each pic on the right

 (DON'T CHEAT!)

MY SCORE OUT OF 20

SEE HOW WELL YOU DID ON P92

JOE HART

MAN. CITY & ENGLAND

POSITION: Keeper
AGE: 24
VALUE: £15 million
DID YOU KNOW?
Joe scored a penalty and saved two in a shootout for England Under-21s in 2009!

MATCH OF THE DAY

GARETH BALE

TOTTENHAM & WALES

POSITION: Winger
AGE: 22
VALUE: £40 million
DID YOU KNOW?
Bale's Champions League hat-trick against Inter Milan last season was his first treble at senior level!

MATCH OF THE DAY

MATCH OF THE DAY

WHO A

Do you ever wonder which type of footballer you'd be?
Take MOTD's test, add up your score, and find out!

Q1 What would your ideal WAG be like?

10PTS Smoking hot and really popular! ☐
8PTS A famous TV star with long dark hair! ☐
6PTS Really cute and likes her private life! ☐
4PTS Anyone who can understand you! ☐
2PTS A nurse, so she can look after you! ☐

Q2 What present do you want for christmas?

10PTS Nike T90 Laser boots to smash in more goals! ☐
8PTS A pair of Adipure boots to help your passing game! ☐
6PTS A goalkeeping tips DVD! ☐
4PTS Any boots that will help you hoof the ball away from goal! ☐
2PTS Bandages and a walking stick! ☐

Q3 What would be your dream moment in a game?

10PTS Scoring an overhead kick against your rivals! ☐
8PTS Hitting a 30-yard screamer into the top corner! ☐
6PTS Saving a penalty in a shootout to win a cup final! ☐
4PTS Blocking a shot at goal with your face! ☐
2PTS Lasting the full 90 minutes without getting injured! ☐

Bag a wonder goal!

Q4 How do you prepare for a game?

10PTS Get pumped up with some loud music! ☐
8PTS Chill by chatting to your mates! ☐
6PTS Repeatedly throw the ball against a wall and catch it! ☐
4PTS Have a massage to keep your legs going! ☐
2PTS Get some more treatment from the physio! ☐

Train to win

northern rock

84

RE YOU?

Q5 What products do you want to advertise on TV?

- 10PTS Wicked computer games! ☐
- 8PTS Smart-looking suits! ☐
- 6PTS Keeper gloves! ☐
- 4PTS Retirement homes! ☐
- 2PTS Hospitals! ☐

Q6 Your team wins a cup — how do you celebvrate?

- 10PTS Go nuts and swing your shirt around your head! ☐
- 8PTS Hug your mates and salute the fans! ☐
- 6PTS High-five your team-mates! ☐
- 4PTS Water! You're knackered and need a drink! ☐
- 2PTS Phone the lads from the treatment room and congratulate them! ☐

Check out the threads!

Old guys need a rest!

22 northern rock.

58

Gatorade

WHICH PLAYER ARE YOU?

54-60 POINTS...
WAYNE ROONEY
You're a goal machine and passionate about football!

42-53 POINTS...
FRANK LAMPARD
You're a wicked, stylish midfielder, liked by everyone!

30-41 POINTS...
JOE HART
You are a top stopper, and your country's No.1!

18-29 POINTS...
JAMIE CARRAGHER
You're a tough defender, but you're getting old now!

12-17 POINTS...
LEDLEY KING
You're always injured. Such a shame because you're a good player!

LUIS SUAREZ

LIVERPOOL & URUGUAY

POSITION: Striker
AGE: 24
VALUE: £30 million
DID YOU KNOW?
Suarez was voted Best Player as he helped Uruguay win the 2011 Copa America!

MATCH OF THE DAY

MATCH OF THE DAY CARTOON FUN!

THE STORY... The MOTD lads have been over to Spain to see Barcelona play live – here's what they found out about them!

What was your fave thing about Barcelona, Al?

Their amazing passing!

They'd fail on Question of Sport though!

How Barça would cope on Sue Barker's quiz...

Which Prem club plays at the Emirates?

Pass!

Pass!

Pass!

XAVI LIONEL MESSI DAVID VILLA

The boys think of the La Liga match they watched...

What impressed you, Gary?

The way they hunt in packs!

I think I saw them on Human Planet on TV!

Pep Guardiola stars in the Human Planet Barça special!

Don't let him go, boys!

We're the **pride** of the jungle!

You're not **lion**, Xavi!

I'm the **mane** man!

They really pressed the opposition!

What are you doing, Lawro?

That pressing talk has given me an idea!

BARSALOWNA

V GETOFF

Lawro has a plan for using Barça's skills...

You've got a lot of slacks!

Lawro's Pants!

They're sorting some **pressing** issues!

Im**press**ive work, lads!

Oi, we're no slacks!

Lawro's Trouser Press

Yeah, we're working as hard as we can!

Pressed Flowers

This is the most de**press**ing job I've ever had!

Pretty Flower Press

THE END!

PAZ AND BEZ'S...
STAR SECRETS!

Paz & Bez are **MOTD** mag and **MOTD** Kickabout's top footy reporters – check out what the stars revealed to them in 2011!

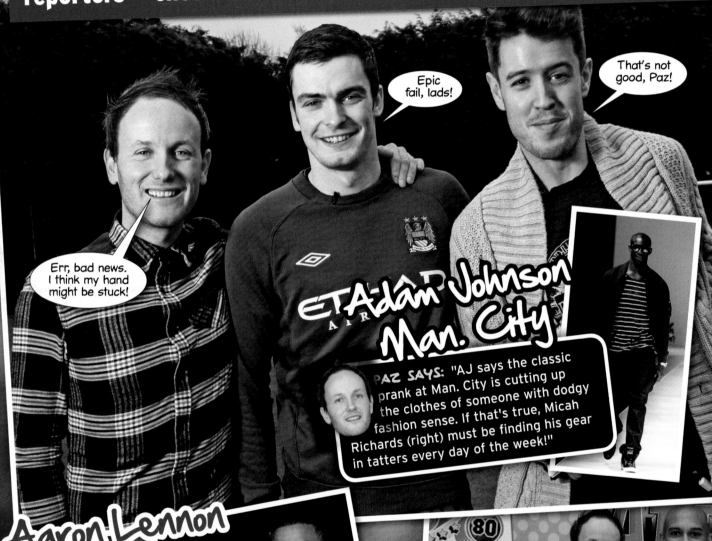

Epic fail, lads!

That's not good, Paz!

Err, bad news. I think my hand might be stuck!

Adam Johnson
Man. City

PAZ SAYS: "AJ says the classic prank at Man. City is cutting up the clothes of someone with dodgy fashion sense. If that's true, Micah Richards (right) must be finding his gear in tatters every day of the week!"

Aaron Lennon
Spurs

BEZ SAYS: "Spurs star Azza told us he's the champ when it comes to computer games with his team-mates. But he went quiet when we said Arsenal's Theo Walcott might be better than him – sounds like these two have some FIFA battles!"

Tim Howard
Everton

BEZ SAYS: "The reason Leighton Baines is now known around the **MOTD** office as the Human Hoover is because team-mate Tim Howard told us he is the king of scoffing sarnies!"

Phil Jones
Man. United

PAZ SAYS: "How do Premier League superstars get their copy of the latest FIFA game? If you're Phil Jones, you send your Mum down to Tesco - that's what the Man. United superkid told us when we went to see him for an exclusive interview!"

Quick, you distract him while I nick a crisp!

Hold-on a minute! Geddit?

Hurry up and take the picture, dude!

Stuart Holden
Bolton

PAZ SAYS: "Stu told us that while the rest of the Bolton squad are busting their gut with extra training sessions, ageing striker Kevin Davies likes to take a rest in the club bath – alright for some, Kev!"

Johan Djourou
Arsenal

BEZ SAYS: "We spent the summer in Africa with Arsenal defender Johan Djourou and we can reveal that man loves to dance! Every time the music started playing in Senegal, we couldn't drag him off the dancefloor!"

Let's have a kickabout!

FUN FOOTY GAME...
EURO CHAMPS!

Try to beat your mate by taking your chances and winning the Champions League final! Take turns rolling a dice – the number it lands on decides what happens. Who'll win this epic clash?

1 You have an early shot at goal!

- **GOAL!** Straight into the top corner!
- **OVER!** Your boss is furious with you!
- **SAVED!** Unlucky, mate – good effort!
- **WIDE!** That almost hit the corner flag!
- **GOAL!** In off the post – BOOM!
- **SAVED!** It comes back to you – roll again!

2 You step up to hit a free-kick!

- **BLOCKED!** Straight in to the wall – roll again!
- **GOAL!** Over the wall and into the net!
- **GOAL!** That ripped the net – the keeper had no chance!
- **OH NO!** You trip over the ball and land on your face!
- **CROSSBAR!** You get the rebound – roll again!
- **SAVED!** Fingertip save from the top stopper!

3 You pick the ball up and run with it!

- **TACKLED!** That didn't go to plan, you numpty!
- **POST!** Great run, but your shot hits the post – roll again!
- **SAVED!** The keeper runs out and blocks your shot!
- **GOAL!** You take on three then chip the keeper!
- **TACKLED!** The centre-back stops you in your tracks!
- **GOAL!** You run past three players then score!

4 You run up to take a penalty!

OVER! That'll land in Iceland – terrible shot!

GOAL! You hit that straight down the middle!

WIDE! Your shot whistles past the post!

GOAL! Right in the corner – impossible to save!

SAVED! The keeper guessed the right way!

GOAL! You slammed that one home!

5 You're put through one-on-one with the keeper!

GOAL! That finish was cooler than a penguin in a fridge!

OVER! You try to chip the keeper but hit it over the bar!

SAVED! The keeper rushes out and blocks your shot!

POST! The ball hits the post and rebounds to you – roll again!

GOAL! You take it around the keeper and knock it into the net!

GOAL! That went straight through the keeper's legs!

6 A corner is whipped in during injury-time! You jump up to meet it!

SAVED! You head it straight at the keeper!

EPIC FAIL! The corner-taker kicks the flag and falls over!

GOAL! You've scored with the last touch of the game!

CLEARED! The defender beats you and clears the danger!

GOAL! You powered that into the net!

POST! You have the ball again – roll again!

FULL-TIME! How many goals did you score? / 6

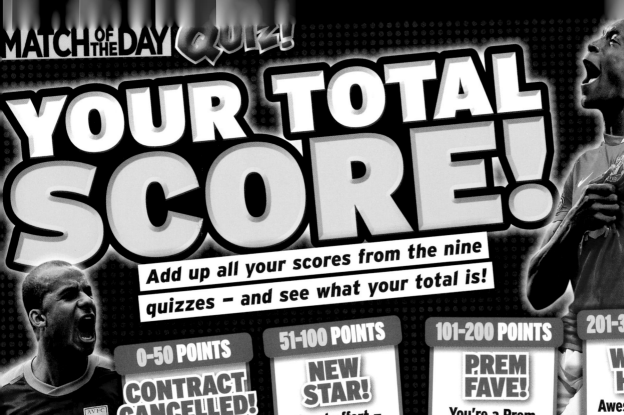

JACK WILSHERE

ARSENAL & ENGLAND

POSITION: Midfielder
AGE: 19
VALUE: £25 million
DID YOU KNOW?
Jack's first ever Prem goal was scored for Bolton when he was on loan there in 2010!

MATCH OF THE DAY

MOTD PREDICTS...
CRAZY TRANSF

Cesc is back, guys!

BALE TO CHELSEA
Chelsea spent months trying to buy Modric from Tottenham this summer – if they bought Bale the Spurs fans would be gutted!

IT WILL HAPPEN! ✓   IT WON'T HAPPEN! ✗

FABREGAS TO ARSENAL
Maybe Cesc will have a stinker for Barca next year and they'll sell him back to Arsenal? Yeah, probably not!

IT WILL HAPPEN! ✓   IT WON'T HAPPEN! ✗

Me and Aguero? Awesome!

ROONEY TO MAN. CITY
City fans would love to snatch Wazza away from United – the club has the cash to do it, too!

IT WILL HAPPEN! ✓   IT WON'T HAPPEN! ✗

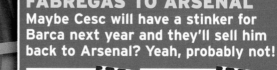

OWEN TO LIVERPOOL
Michael used to bang in the goals for The Reds – and we reckon he could do a job for them again!

IT WILL HAPPEN! ✓   IT WON'T HAPPEN! ✗

94